Steph Tranter

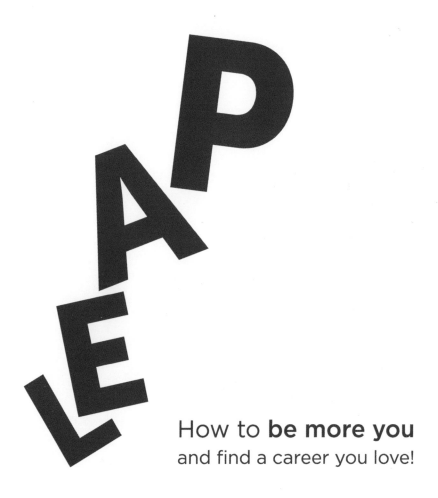

How to **be more you**
and find a career you love!

About
the author

Steph Tranter is a Hybrid Executive Coach, merging the worlds of coaching and therapy. What makes Steph different to other executive coaches is that she blends her practical experience of having worked in the corporate world, with deeper insights from psychology and therapy. Steph is neither your bog-standard executive coach, nor is she a counsellor; she is a hybrid of the two.

In 2011, Steph took her own LEAP from the corporate world into self-employment, and has been running her executive coaching business since then. She primarily works with c-suite and executive directors, and has a broad experience across a range of industries and sizes of organisations, from small Tech start-ups, to large well-established global brands like Harrods, Tesco and WeWork. She has also worked with charities, public sector organisations including two Police forces, and within the Sports industry, including UK Sport, The Sport and Recreation Alliance, and the British Olympic Equestrian Team.

Steph has a background in Retail and Leadership Development, holds a BSC in Psychology, an MA in Visual Communication, and a Coaching qualification from Oxford Brookes University, endorsed by the European Mentoring and Coaching Council.

If you want to hear how Steph's clients have applied the tools, techniques and approaches in this book, then check out Steph's **Podcast - Warts 'n' All Leadership**, which can be found on all major podcast platforms.

Praise for Leap!

"*For anyone feeling a little stuck or lost, LEAP offers many simple tools along with practical guidance to help navigate many of life's challenges*"
GAVIN OATTES - **Bestselling author of 'Life Will See You Now', International Keynote speaker, award winning Comedian and MD of Tree of Knowledge**

"*So many people fall into a job or career which they find dull, boring, unpleasant and thoroughly unfulfilling. Too many people feel Sunday night blues with work on Monday looming. If this is you then LEAP! can change your life. The beauty of LEAP! is that it's a super easy to read, logical step by step approach to transforming your career and life. Through the use of simple and easy techniques backed up by proven scientific thinking Steph takes you through a journey of understanding yourself, opening your eyes, resetting your horizon, changing your perspectives and realising your dreams. The only constraint is you! Don't spend the rest of your life in a career you don't love. Read LEAP! and take your first step to changing your life for the better*"
MARK THOMAS - **Vice President Talent Acquisition & Development – Abcam**

"*I love the simplicity, the style, and the structure of Steph's book. I love how Steph gives you the opportunity to start making a plan from the moment you start reading LEAP, so that you can get clear on why you're reading this book and what you're looking to get out of it. I found that I could quickly read the book from front to back, but I could also very easily dip in and out of any chapter and still get some gems out of it without having read any of the other chapters. A great book. Well done Steph*"
BRAD SOLOMAN - **Founder, CEO, Coach, Podcaster and Platform Speaker at The CTG Group**

"Perfectly practical in every way! Leap into this book - it's powerful, practical and supportive at each and every stage. Steph has created a personal framework to support and guide you through challenging and thought provoking questions to be your best you. Loved it."

RACHEL PARSONAGE **- CEO - KMI Brands. Recognised as one of the top 50 Most Ambitious Business leaders in the UK**

"LEAP is accessible, relatable, easy to understand, and not overstuffed. It's all essential reading, and has some of the most poignant, perfect and perfectly located motivational quotes I've ever seen in a book. Highly recommended."

DR PAUL BREWERTON **- Doctor of Psychology, Founder and Chair of Strengthscope, Strategic Director at You Collective**

"LEAP! Provides a practical approach to making life choices whether you are starting out, seeking your next chapter or even considering your route to retirement! Steph Tranter is an accomplished coach who brings her ideas to life in this book as though she is sitting right there next to you. This is next level coaching in that the destination is determined by the reader, with Steph's voice, exercises, and models as your guide. Each chapter takes you further along your journey of discovery, with reflective exercises that provide an incremental approach for sustainable personal change.My daughter has just changed her mind about her career and LEAP! has helped her think about her next choices - so it's certainly a book for the whole family!!!"

PAUL HILLAN **- Head of Organisational Learning at The Open University**

"LEAP helps people navigate their future using evidence based tools in a step by step way. I've had the privilege of working with Steph and delighted to see her passion for people come through in this simple and excellent read"

JANE STORM **- Group People Director, EasyJet plc**

Dedicated to my cat Felix, who for 12 years was by my side through every leap I have taken in my personal life and my career, and who took his final leap at the time of writing this book.

Though no one can go back and make a brand new start, anyone can start from NOW **and make a brand new ending!**

———

Carl Bard
Writer & Editor

Illustrations and graphics created through a collaboration between Steph Tranter, and many of the team at Alive with Ideas, including Andy Davies, Ellie Luckett, Rob Leech, Valentina Zagaglia and David (Stan) Stanley.

Front cover designed by Alan Oram, Founder and Director at Alive with Ideas.

Contents

I've learned that making a 'LIVING' is not the same as 'making A LIFE'

———

Maya Angelou
Writer, Poet & Activist

Introduction
Getting unstuck

Introduction
Getting unstuck

HOW DID YOU GET TO BE IN THE JOB YOU'RE IN?

When clients come to me because they're at a crossroads in their career and feeling stuck, I ask them how they got to be in the job or career they are in.

The answer I usually get is:
"I'm not really sure, I just sort of fell into this career."

This seems to be a common theme with the clients I coach, and whilst some of us get lucky and fall into roles and careers that we love, most of us don't. Yet we allow ourselves to continue to be swept along the path we've fallen onto, when in the privacy of our own hearts, we know this isn't where we want to be.

The problem is we don't know where we do want to be. We just know it's not here. There's also a feeling that to make a change now would be an UNNECESSARY LEAP into the unknown. It would risk everything you've worked so hard to get, and for what? Just a pipe dream? Or something you might not be that good at anyway?

So, you feel stuck.
You know you want things to change, but for some reason you're not making the change.

WHY YOU FEEL STUCK

The clients I work with tell me they feel stuck or don't take the leap they want to take, because of one of three reasons:

1. They don't really know what they want
2. They don't think they can get what they want
3. They don't know where to start or can't think clearly

However, from my experience of working with these clients, **those are not the real reasons!**

THE REAL REASONS PEOPLE GET STUCK:

- They **underestimate** the power of their **NATURAL STRENGTHS** and the unique value they already offer

- They've not spent **PRODUCTIVE THINKING** time working out what they want and what's important to them

- Their emotions (**fear and worry mainly**) are clouding their thinking and judgement.

HOW DO I KNOW THESE ARE THE REAL REASONS?

Because once these reasons are addressed, I see more people getting unstuck. I see it becoming easier for them to do something tangible towards making a change. After tackling these issues with my clients, they then develop the clarity and confidence to take their leaps!

WHAT DO I MEAN BY 'PRODUCTIVE THINKING'?

We often believe that we have been seriously considering the leap we want to take, making plans, and rationally discounting ideas.

When in fact all we've been doing is pondering over a few repetitive thoughts in our head, or sharing some vague ideas with a friend. That's not productive thinking.

Productive thinking is about prioritising dedicated and focused time to doing some practical exploration and investigation into who you are, what you really want, and how you could make it all happen.

HOW CAN THIS BOOK HELP?

This book is organised into chapters that will help you to do that productive thinking, and address each of the real reasons that are keeping your feet firmly stuck on the ground right now.

Chapter 1 and Chapter 2 will help you to identify what makes you unique and the value you already add just by being who you already are.

Chapter 3 will help you to do some productive thinking about what you want, why you want those things and what's important to you.

Chapter 4 will help you to identify and overcome any fears you have that are stopping you from taking the leap you want to take.

Chapter 5 will help you to create a practical plan that will fit into your life so that you are able to stick to it, as well as enjoy it.

BACKGROUND TO MY PROCESS AND TOOLS

I describe myself as a Hybrid Executive Coach because my approach merges the worlds of coaching and therapy. I blend the practical, future-focused, goal-based approach of corporate coaching, with the more in depth, person-centred approach of therapy. I believe coaching someone around their career can only be effective if you look at the whole person, not just them at work. So you will find a blend of this approach throughout the book.

With the exception of Strengthscope , all of the tools in this book are either my own creation, or existing tools that I've adapted to make them simpler or more practical.

 This symbol indicates the tools in each chapter of this book.

 This symbol indicates where you can make a note of any insights you've had or actions you'd like to take at the end of each chapter.

There are 12 tools for you to complete, and space is provided for you to work through these tools directly within the book. If however, you would prefer to use a separate copy of the tool, then please contact me. My details can be found on p.144.

I aim to make working with me and working through this book to feel like you are simply working with a skilled friend.

But you know YOU better than I do. I'm just going to ask some questions and give you some structure and tools to help facilitate, organise, clarify and at times challenge your thoughts and feelings. So as you work through the exercises, trust in your own judgement. As I said, you know you better than anyone else does!

HOW THIS APPROACH CAN WORK

Amy was feeling stuck. She had enjoyed working in the same organisation for ten years, progressing into management for five of those years. But when I met Amy, she had become disillusioned with her job and the organisation. She lacked energy and motivation, and suffered from anxiety brought on by work.

But she had no idea what to do about it, or what she could do about it. She'd lost confidence in who she was, what she was able to do, and even in her own ability to know and decide what she wanted. She confessed that all she really wanted was for me to give her the answers and tell her what to do.

But of course I wasn't going to do that. I worked with Amy for six sessions over six months, taking her through many of the tools and approaches in this book. This resulted in Amy uncovering and sometimes rediscovering who she was, what she wanted and what was important to her.

By the end of the coaching she no longer felt stuck, anxious, and lost. She now understood, and more importantly, valued her strengths and natural qualities, which gave her an increased sense of self-belief. She was also clearer on the sort of job she wanted to do, and company she wanted to work for.

So much so that just before our last session, she did something that she previously would not have had the confidence or clarity to do. She applied for a job in a company that was more aligned to her passions and values, and to her amazement was offered it.

THIS IS WHAT AMY SAID ABOUT THE COACHING:

"When I met Steph, I wasn't necessarily in the best headspace, I had already tried a previous form of coaching which wasn't the right fit for me, and so I wasn't 100% sold on this working.

I went into the sessions hoping to be given the majority of answers to fix my problems (I know coaching doesn't work this way) but at the time this is what I thought I needed.

Steph's coaching methods felt like taking a full breath again, it gave me the space and confidence to not only explore how I was feeling at the time, and what I wanted to do in my career, but also where I wanted to work and how important that is as well.

The tools and tasks helped me to understand myself better, finding a positive outlet for my emotions and pausing when I felt overwhelmed.

Whilst the process wasn't easy, Steph didn't just give me the answers like I wanted, she helped me to work through everything myself with nudging and support from her in a relaxed and friendly environment."

Tools in this book

TOOL 1

MY LIFE SO FAR

Helps you to create a picture of you at your best

p.40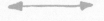

TOOL 2

MY VALUES

Helps you to articulate the key qualities that are important to you

p.45

TOOL 3

WHO ANNOYS ME

Helps you to dig deeper into understanding your core values

p.47

TOOL 4

WHO INSPIRES ME

Helps you to explore what's really important to you

p.48

TOOL 5

MY TOP VALUES

Helps you to summarise the values that are most important to you

p.50

TOOL 6

THE VALUE I ALREADY ADD

Helps you to get clear what others see as your natural strengths

p.58

TOOL 7

MY PASSIONS AND INTERESTS

Helps you to identify what gives you energy and what you love to do

p.74

TOOL 8

MY IDEAL LIFE

Helps you to structure how to dream

p.77

TOOL 9

ME AT MY BEST

Helps you to summarise what you look like at your best

p.82

TOOL 10

CREATING A PLAN I CAN STICK TO

Helps you to ensure your plan will fit into your daily life

p.126

TOOL 11

REVIEWING MY OBJECTIVES

Helps you to see what you've achieved and what's left to do

p.130

BONUS TOOL

PROS AND CONS +

Helps you to choose from many ideas

p.132

Making my plan

WHAT DO YOU WANT TO GET OUT OF THIS BOOK?

One of the aims of this book is to provide you with an opportunity to identify some practical steps towards taking the leap you want to take, not just offer up theories and ideas. To support you to do that, at the end of each chapter there is a 'Making my plan' section for you to make notes about any key insights you've had, and actions you want to take as a result of those insights.

The first action to take (which is what I do with all my coaching clients at the beginning of working together) is to identify your objectives, i.e. what do you want to get out of reading this book? To help you with this, I've included some of the common objectives that my clients often have.

Have a look at the objectives below and tick as many as are appropriate to you.

YOUR OBJECTIVES FOR READING THIS BOOK

By the end of this book, I would like to:

- ☐ Be clear where I want to go next in my career
- ☐ Know how I can do more work that I love
- ☐ Understand my strengths better
- ☐ Gain confidence in who I am
- ☐ Understand what gives me energy
- ☐ Understand what I'm passionate about
- ☐ Build my confidence to go after the career I want
- ☐ Overcome what's stopping me take the leap
- ☐ Decide which career option to take next
- ☐ Make a plan to help me take the leap

In the space below, make a note of any other objectives you might have.

By the end of this book, I would like to:

We are all born
with immense
NATURAL TALENTS,
but too few people
discover what
they are, and even
fewer develop
them properly.

———

Sir Ken Robinson
Author, Speaker & Government Advisor

Chapter 1

Who am I?
And why don't I already know?

Chapter 1
Who am I?
And why don't I already know?

WHO ARE YOU?

When you talk about wanting to know who you are, what I suspect you mean is that you want to know what makes you unique. What's special or different about you? What does it mean to be you?

This can often hit us out of the blue one morning when we wake up and think:

"What am I doing with my life?
How did I end up here?
Why am I so unhappy?
Why do I feel so trapped, constrained, confused?
Why am I stuck?
What happened?"

I'll tell you what happened.

HOW DID YOU END UP HERE?

I appreciate this may not be true for everyone, but for many of us we were once carefree, creative, curious children, with the desire to explore, to create, and to express our ideas. Life was full of wonder, fun, intrigue and excitement. We explored the world without the worry of being judged, or rejected, or the pressure of having to pay the mortgage.

But then life got in the way. We had to get a sensible bill paying career. We had to keep up with our peers. We had to grow up!

NO WONDER WE LOSE SIGHT OF WHO WE ARE

From our early teenage years onwards, we progressively lose sight of who we are, what our natural strengths are, and what we love to do. We get hijacked by our hormones in our teens, and begin to worry more about fitting in than following our dreams. We get either catastrophic career advice, or no advice when we're choosing key subjects to study or paths to follow, and so end up going down the 'sensible' route, rather than the route we truly want.

Yet despite our teenage years being a really confusing and turbulent time for us, it's at these times we are asked to make some big decisions about what we want to do with our lives.

I mean, who on earth designed it this way?

"I know", they said, "let's wait until children get to that stage in their lives when they constantly get hijacked by confusing emotions, struggling with what life is about and how to fit in. When they are full of internal conflicts of who they are and how to cope with life.

Then, when these teenagers are at their most vulnerable and fragile, let's ask them to make some really big decisions that will affect the rest of their lives.

We'll ask them 'what do you want to do with your life?'

Then we'll offer up a really limited list of subjects to choose from, and too bad if they're not interested in them, or that good at them.

We'll push these kids away from what they really want, because we won't even put that on the table, we won't offer it up as an option. Not because we're mean, just because we're constrained by our own rules, and didn't even know it was an option."

WHAT WE NEEDED WASN'T OFFERED AT SCHOOL

Where on the syllabus at school were the subjects on how to find out what your natural strengths are, or what you really love to do, or what makes you uniquely you?

Why were Maths, Science and English given more space on the curriculum than Sports, Music and Art? Why was there such a limited set of subjects to choose from and learn about?

I guess what I'm saying here is that it's really no wonder that we end up so far away from who we are and what we love to do.

So maybe don't beat yourself up so much about how you have ended up stuck in the 'sensible life'. You were hardly set up to succeed. I don't mean that people deliberately made you take a path they knew would ultimately make you unhappy. I just don't think many of us were given the right skills, knowledge or support needed to set us up to succeed in a career and life completely aligned to who we are and what we love to do.

THE BIGGEST PROBLEM WITH THIS STORY

The biggest problem with this story is that we become good at being sensible.

A solid career, nice house, decent salary. We strive and strive, blind-sided by our striving, until that day we wake up and realise we're just not happy. There must be more to life than this!

And a quiet, but persistent voice in your head keeps whispering –

...there is more to me than this.

What's more, being successful at 'being sensible' has made it feel even harder to take a leap into being who you truly are, as well as a leap into a life you really want to live.

THIS WHOLE STORY WAS CERTAINLY TRUE FOR ME

I was never really sure what I wanted to do with my life, and by my late teens started to really struggle with the whole point to it all. I didn't want to just grow up, go to work, earn money, get married, buy a house, have a family, retire… and then die. I also didn't want to wait until I retired and was at my least mentally and physically fit to finally start doing what I loved.

I'm not saying that the path of working hard and earning money to raise a family isn't meaningful, it just wasn't for me.

I wanted a purpose and a meaning, but had no idea what it takes to have a meaningful life, or how to make the best decisions to get there. The routes mapped out and offered up to me just weren't right.

I wasn't one of those people lucky enough to be totally certain on what I wanted to do, and I didn't stand out as having any particular skill in any one thing. I've later realised that I didn't stand out in any one thing, because the thing I stand out in, wasn't given as an option at school.

So almost by default, I got caught up in following the sensible route and ended up turning my part-time Saturday job on the checkouts at Tesco (that helped fund my way through university studying a subject I really enjoyed) into a full-time management training scheme.

Eleven years later, I found I had continued to live my life by default rather than by design. I was still at Tesco having progressed through the ranks and achieved a bill paying, yet on the whole, unfulfilling career. I had lost sight of who I was, and was the furthest away I had ever been from knowing, let alone doing, what I love to do.

My sensible, secure, and safe life was also keeping me too busy and too tired to do anything about it.

LIFTING THE VEIL OF THE SENSIBLE LIFE

That wonderfully curious, creative and unique individual, full of ideas, and an interest in expressing and exploring those ideas, is still within you.

They are just hidden under the veil of your 'sensible' life.

You may have lost your way, but you can find it again.

You **can** get clarity on what you want.

You **can** get the confidence to be yourself and do what you love.

You **can** get that curiosity and creativity back in your life.

From the safety, security and certainty of your current life, you **can** take that LEAP into what right now feels like an unsafe, insecure, uncertain place you've been educated out of believing to be possible.

I know you can do it, because I did it! And so too have many of my coaching clients. All of whom started out with low confidence, minimal resources and no clue as to where to begin (that describes where I was too). In this book, I'm going to show you what my clients and I did to help us to take our LEAPs!

The extracts on the next page are from a quote by Marianne Williamson (made famous by Nelson Mandela) which summarise perfectly the essence of what this book is about.

Our deepest fear is not
that we are inadequate,
Our deepest fear is that we are
powerful beyond measure.
It is our light, not our darkness
that most frightens us.

We ask ourselves,
'who am I to be: brilliant,
gorgeous, talented, fabulous?'
Actually, who are you not to be?
Your playing small does not
serve the world.

There is nothing enlightened
about shrinking so that other people
won't feel insecure around you.
We are all meant to shine,
as children do.

And as we let our own light shine,
we unconsciously give other people
permission to do the same.
As we are liberated from our
own fear, our presence
automatically liberates others.

———

Marianne Williamson
Author, Spiritual Leader, Activist

Making my plan

MY REFLECTIONS AND INSIGHTS

Make a note below of any reflections or insights you've had from reading the Introduction and Chapter 1.

Did anything particularly resonate with you?
How do you feel having read the Introduction and Chapter 1?

My reflections, insights, thoughts or feelings:

MY ACTIONS

Make a note below of any actions you would like to take as a result of the reflections and insights you captured after reading the Introduction and Chapter 1. For example, your action might be to plan time in your diary each week to complete the tools in this book.

Actions I want to take:

**You are ALREADY
standing on a
mountain of value.
Your story is valuable.
Your EXPERIENCE
is unique!**

Daniel Priestley
Entrepreneur

Chapter 2

**How to uncover
what makes me unique**

Chapter 2
How to uncover what makes me unique

WHAT MAKES YOU UNIQUE?

I believe what makes you unique is a wonderful combination of your natural strengths, your developed skills, your values, beliefs, experiences, passions, interests, influences and where you get your energy from. But has anyone ever taught you how to identify these things?

I suspect most workshops, development activities, or training courses you've attended (and let's not forget school here), have not focused on what makes you uniquely you. I suspect they've been more focused on helping you to learn a technical skill or fix your personal weaknesses. Not about what your natural strengths are and how to identify what's important to you, or what makes you unique, or how you add value just by being you. But as Daniel Priestley says in his book 'Key Person of Influence':

"You are already standing on a mountain of value".

So how do you uncover that mountain of value?
Well, I'm glad you asked.

On the next page is a tool that will help you to understand yourself better, and start to explore what that mountain of value is made up of.

The tool is called My life so far and the aim of this tool is to help you to discover any themes or patterns around what you look like when you're at your best, as well as what needs to be in place for you to be at your best. This will help you to see what your mountain of value looks like, as well as how you can continue to use that mountain of value in the future.

You may need to come back to this exercise a few times as you read through this book, as further memories of times when you've been at your best might pop up as you work through the other exercises.

Tool 1

MY LIFE SO FAR

Think of key moments in your life since about the age of 10 (personal and work based) when you felt energised, happy and possibly even fulfilled and successful. List them here:

Now think of key moments when you felt drained, unhappy or unfulfilled and not successful. List them here:

Now plot your moments onto the timeline below. You may want to draw this onto a separate piece of paper to give you more room. Plot the moments either above or below the timeline depending on how happy or energised you felt. Plot your happiest and most energising moments above the line. The higher you plot, the happier they are. Plot your least happy or energising moments below the line. The lower you plot, the less happy they are.

YOUR ENERGISING OR HAPPY EXPERIENCES

TIMELINE

NOW

10 YEARS OLD

YOUR DRAINING OR UNHAPPY EXPERIENCES

Tool 1

MY LIFE SO FAR

Look at your high points (above the line) and answer the following questions:

What were you doing that gave you energy?

What strengths were you using?

What values were you living by?

What environments were you in?

What sort of people were you with?

What experiences did these times give you and what did you learn about yourself?

Look at your low points (below the line) and answer the following questions:

What were you doing that drained you?

What strengths were you unable to use?

What values were missing?

What environments were you in?

What sort of people were you with?

What experiences did these times give you, and what did you learn about yourself?

HOW DO YOU WORK OUT WHAT YOUR VALUES ARE?

When you were completing the *My life so far* exercise, you may have found that it wasn't always that easy to spot your values. That's because values are often so ingrained into the way we think and behave that we don't always notice or articulate them.

However, being clear on your values can help you to navigate your career towards environments, companies, cultures, people and activities that allow you to be the person you want to be. This next section and set of tools will help you to more easily identify and articulate your values.

SO WHAT ARE VALUES AND HOW DO YOU SPOT THEM?

Values are the **qualities** that **guide** our **behaviour**.

Values define how we want to behave, or believe is the right way for us to behave. There's no right or wrong way to describe your values. Sometimes it's a word, sometimes a phrase. In *Tool 2* there are some common words people have used to describe their values. This is not an exhaustive list, but it is a good starting point to think about values.

Can you identify 5-10 values that stand out for you?

It might help to look the words up in a dictionary and see what resonates. Conversely, it can sometimes help to cross out the words that definitely don't resonate with you first. If there are any other words or phrases not on the opposite page that you feel describe your values, make a note of them below:

Other words or phrases that describe my values:

Tool 2

MY VALUES

Circle up to ten words that stand out as important to you.

RISK

FUN

TRUST

COLLABORATION

GROWTH

INTEGRITY

CURIOSITY

CONNECTION

SERVICE

OPENNESS

CHALLENGE

COMMON VALUE WORDS

PASSION

FREEDOM

BELONGING

HONESTY

LOVE

TEAM WORK

PERSISTENCE

JUSTICE

COMMITMENT

HUMILITY

LEARNING

KINDNESS

COURAGE

RESPECT

NON-JUDGEMENT

HUMOUR

FAIRNESS

FORGIVENESS

ACHIEVEMENT

TAKING A CLOSER LOOK AT VALUES

If you found it hard to see your values just from the words on the previous page, there are a couple of other techniques you can use to get clearer on what your values are. Whether you struggled or not, I'd recommend these next techniques in Tool 3 - Who annoys me, and Tool 4 - Who inspires me.

To demonstrate how the technique works, you will see below my own example of Tool 3 - Who annoys me and what that tells me about my values.

My example of
Tool 3 - Who annoys me

I often get really annoyed when someone cuts me up on the motorway.

When I explored the reason why this is, and what value this behaviour was treading on, I realised that I get annoyed because the person had no consideration for me.

So the value for me here is:
To be considerate of others

Tool 3

WHO ANNOYS ME, AND WHAT THAT TELLS ME ABOUT MY VALUES.

The values you hold dear are often absent from those people who annoy you or make you angry.

Therefore, one exercise that can help you to identify your values, is to think about what it is about someone that annoys or angers you.

So who annoys you? And what values do you think this highlights?

Complete the following questions.

Think about at least 2-3 people who completely get on your nerves or whose behaviour irks you.

1. What do they do or say that annoys you?

2. What do you interpret this behaviour to mean about them?

3. What value or values of yours do you think this behaviour is highlighting?

Tool 4

WHO INSPIRES ME, AND WHAT THAT TELLS ME ABOUT MY VALUES.

Another technique to gain insight into what's important to you, is to consider the opposite types of people from those you ranted about in the previous exercise.

This time think about the people you admire, are inspired by, or just simply respect, and why you admire them, are inspired by them or respect them.

This might be someone famous, a friend or a family member, but they are likely to be someone you really want to be around, or you like reading about or following on social media.

This is my example of Who inspires me **to help show how the exercise works.**

	Who	Qualities
1	Steve Jobs	Creativity, Belief in his ideas, thought differently
2	Princess Diana	Authentic, Challenged the norm, Not afraid to be different
3	Ken Robinson	Passion and Humor, Challenges the school system, Champions creativity

My themes

Creativity
Thinking/being different
Challenging the system

Identify three people and the qualities they have that you really admire, respect, or are inspired by.

Who inspires me

	Who	Qualities
1		
2		
3		

Write any themes in here

Tool 5

MY TOP VALUES

Look back over the last four exercises and try to summarise your top six values. Write your top values in the bubbles below as a record of what you've discovered about yourself so far.

SO WHAT DO YOU DO WITH ALL THIS INFO?

In this chapter you have started to identify several aspects that make up a picture of you at your best!

So far there's been a deliberate focus on clarifying your values. That's because knowing your values not only has a big impact on where you go next in your career, but also on how you want to live your life as a whole.

THE EXTRA VALUE YOU GET FROM KNOWING YOUR VALUES

Our values can also be our **anchors** during uncertain times. When thinking about your future, you will naturally be faced with a lot of uncertainty, as well as factors that are completely out of your control. This can be very unsettling. However, knowing your values during these times of uncertainty can help you to focus on what is in your control, and that's your behaviour. Your values can guide you towards how you want to behave, so even if you're not certain of what will happen, you can be certain on how you want to behave in the process of getting there.

In this chapter, you've also uncovered what activities energise you, and what experiences make up the high points in your life. This information is useful because it shows you what you love doing, and therefore where you could take your career.

On pages 82 and 83, you can start to create a summary of everything you are discovering about yourself. There are ten hexagonal sections to complete, and each has a page reference next to it so you can find the information to enter into that hexagon. You have enough information now to start to fill in the following sections:

1. Activities that energise me
2. High points (Personal)
3. High points (Work)
4. Environments I thrive in
5. People I thrive around
6. My top values

FILL ME IN
ON PAGES
82 AND 83

HOW CAN I BE SURE WHAT MY STRENGTHS ARE?

In the My life so far exercise, you were asked to spot what strengths you were using at your high points, as well as what strengths you weren't able to use at your low points. Knowing your strengths and focusing much more on your strengths than on your weaknesses, is a core part of the process in helping you to **be more you**! If you struggled to fully identify and articulate your strengths, then the following information could help.

A MINDSET SHIFT - THE STRENGTHS APPROACH

The strengths approach that I use with my clients provides a complete mindset shift from the traditional way we view ourselves and how we approach our personal and professional development. This approach came from a body of scientific research carried out within the field of positive psychology.

WHAT IS POSITIVE PSYCHOLOGY?

Most of the time when research is carried out in the general field of psychology, the focus tends to be on what goes wrong for us psychologically. For example, when we suffer mental health issues or personality disorders. Psychology research therefore tends to focus on helping people to overcome any struggles they have with functioning in day to day life.

This is represented on the Flourishing Spectrum on the opposite page as going from 'Struggling' to 'Surviving', and is where the focus usually is within counselling and therapy. So traditional psychology research is clearly very valuable and very needed.

However, in the late 1990s, Martin Seligman, the President of the American Psychological Association, suggested that to only carry out research into psychological disease, deficit and disorder, meant that nearly 50% of human experience was being missed. Seligman identified that there was a gap in research about when things go right, or when people are living fulfilling and meaningful lives.

As a result, the positive psychology movement began, which in turn produced a body of research focused on understanding more about the science of when things go right in life.

One of the findings in positive psychology research was that understanding and playing to your natural strengths can help you move from 'Surviving' (that's often where the majority of us live, functioning ok in day to day but not always happy) to thriving, or absolutely 'Smashing it' in life. You can see this represented on the Flourishing Spectrum below:

The Flourishing Spectrum

The strengths approach can get you:

From here..   **..to here**

Struggling
Struggling to function
in day to day life

Surviving
Can function but
not always happy

Smashing it
Thriving, fulfilled,
creative, alive

BUT SHOULDN'T YOU TRY TO FIX YOUR WEAKNESSES?

The idea of focusing on your weaknesses in order to improve yourself, permeates all aspects of our working lives. There is an underlying belief within this approach that we should be good at everything, and perfectly well-rounded. If we're not, then we won't be successful. Cover all bases, so to speak, just in case.

If you look at job descriptions, they are written for rounded people. Performance reviews and development conversations encourage you to improve in your weaker areas in order to make you rounded.

But, being asked to become good at everything is demonstrably demoralising, not to mention arguably impossible.

It's no surprise that the weakness model is rife in our lives, because it's been around since our school days. If you look at where the attention of your teachers and parents went when you were at school, they honed in on the subjects where you received your lowest grades, and fixated on how you can make them better. Rather than focusing on opportunities to enable you to do even more of the things that you are naturally great at.

You're not taught from an early age how to make your natural strengths stronger. You're not taught how to **be more you**. You are taught how to be rounded. How to be sensible.

No human being is good at everything, no human being is rounded, and no human being should be influenced into becoming rounded either!

Play to your strengths, ditch trying to be rounded.

We are all unique individuals with a unique set of strengths. The more we push ourselves into this 'rounded' category, the further away we are going to get from who we actually are.

So, in short, no, I don't believe you need to fix your weaknesses. I think you've spent your whole life doing that. Isn't it time for a different approach? Isn't it time to address the balance of where you've been focusing and get to know your strengths better?

WHY WE STRUGGLE TO IDENTIFY OUR STRENGTHS

Sadly, because of the general focus on weaknesses, we rarely notice our strengths, or we take our strengths for granted. They come so naturally to us that we don't notice them or sometimes don't even value them.

When we use a natural strength we often just assume:
"...doesn't everyone think like this? act like this? question this?"

The answer is **no!**

Your strengths tend to show up in the questions you ask, or where your focus goes. Not everyone generates the same questions in their minds, or directs their attention to the same areas of focus.

A person with an efficiency strength might ask:
"How can this be better organised?"

A person with a creativity strength might ask:
"I wonder what would happen if we put these two things together?"

A person with an empathy strength might ask:
"How is this going to make someone feel?"

These questions happen so naturally and quickly that we don't always appreciate they are the result of our strengths. But if someone doesn't have an empathy strength, they may never ask the question "how is this going to make someone feel?"

So the beauty of the strengths approach is that it can help shine a light on the things that we dismiss as *'just being me'* or *'just what I do'*. When in fact what you do, is very unique to you, and very needed.

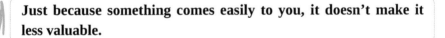

Just because something comes easily to you, it doesn't make it less valuable.

Because our strengths come so naturally to us, we can often believe they are less valuable than something that takes hard work to do. That's because we generally value the things that take hard work. Also, because of the continual focus on our weaknesses, we've sadly learned to place a disproportionate amount of value on the qualities we don't have.

But if something comes easily to you, it is still valuable, because that quality may not come easily to others, and so they (and the world) are likely to need it from you.

There is another mindset shift here. To go from thinking about 'value' not in terms of how hard something is to do, but in terms of how needed it is.

HOW DO YOU FIND OUT WHAT YOUR STRENGTHS ARE?

There are several exercises that can help you to start to spot your strengths. Here are 3 ways to help you to find out what your strengths are:

1. Go back to the My life so far exercise and re-look at the times when you were happy and energised. Then identify what you added to those situations that others didn't. What qualities did you have or behaviours were you able to display that helped the situation?

Make notes below:

In the high points of your My life so far exercise, what qualities did you add, or behaviours did you display that others didn't?

2. We often get frustrated by people who don't do what we feel is obvious. It is obvious to you because you have a strength that enables you to see it. But it's not obvious to them because they don't have that strength. So think back to times when something felt obvious to you but not to others, and identify what strength you feel you had that enabled you to see what others couldn't.

What seemed obvious to you, that wasn't obvious to others, and what strength do you think this means you have?

3. There are several personality profiling tools that can help you to identify your strengths. The best one I use, and the only one of it's kind to be endorsed by the British Psychological Society, is **Strengthscope®**. You can find out more about Strengthscope® by visiting their website **www.strengthscope.com**.

If you would like to complete the Strengthscope® questionnaire to discover your strengths, then please get in touch with me (you can find my contact details at the end of this book on p.144).

To emphasise just how unique you are, the people at Strengthscope® found:

The likelihood of you getting **the same** top 7 **strengths** in the same **order** as someone else is:

①in
1.7 billion!©

*This is how **unique** you are!*

Tool 6

THE VALUE I ALREADY ADD

This exercise will help you see what others value about you, and will give you further insights into your natural strengths. It always feels difficult to ask for feedback from others, even if you've done it many times before. However most people are delighted to help, especially when you ask such positive questions as the ones in this exercise.

So if you are feeling brave enough, actually even if you're not, do the following exercise and it will enable you to get an insight into what others value in you. What you'll find is that other people are usually much better than you at articulating what's great about you, and what your strengths are. By carrying out this exercise it will also become quite apparent that what others value in you is also what you value in yourself.

So give this a go. I've never had anyone be disappointed with the results!

Write down the names of 5-10 people who know you well. Make it a mix of colleagues, friends and family members.

1 ....   6 ....

2 ....   7 ....

3 ....   8 ....

4 ....   9 ....

5 ....   10 ....

Ask each of these people to answer the following questions:

1. What 2-3 qualities do you most value in me?

2. Is there a picture, image or cartoon character (basically anything visual) that best describes me? (if so, can you send it to me, or a link to it please)

3. Is there a song, book or movie that you feel best describes me? If so, can you tell me what it is and why you chose it?

Once you get back all the answers, see if you can spot any themes about your strengths. Try to identify 3-6 themes that would represent the words from the feedback, and label each Strength Bucket on the following pages with those themes.

For example, this is how I created themes from some of the feedback I received from those questions:

My strengths buckets

Also make a note here of any songs, books, movies or visuals that you were pleased to receive, or that really resonated with you.

Tool 6

Name and fill your Strengths Buckets:

You can now fill in the section on your top strengths on p.83

Here are some extra Strengths Buckets:

You can now fill in the section on your top strengths on p.83

Making my plan

MY REFLECTIONS AND INSIGHTS

Make a note below of any reflections or insights you've had from reading Chapter 2.

Did anything particularly resonate with you?
How do you feel having read Chapter 2?

My reflections, insights, thoughts or feelings:

MY ACTIONS

Make a note below of any actions you would like to take as a result of the reflections and insights you captured after reading Chapter 2.

Actions I want to take:

Kind words from my clients about the tools and techniques in this chapter.

"I had been feeling stuck and unfulfilled in my role, but using the tools in this chapter helped me realise that the problem wasn't with me, it was the environment. This massive breakthrough completely reframed the way I think about myself professionally. Using the comprehensive exercises in this chapter, Steph helped me understand my natural strengths and how to identify the right environment for me. I went from feeling like a perpetual misfit, to gaining clarity on the process and steps to find a better-suited environment. Thanks to Steph, I landed a new role that I'm genuinely excited about and pays significantly more than my prior role. My career no longer feels stale, but purposeful."

KUDZAYI CHAKAHWATA - Worldwide Data and Technology Director - Publicis Groupe

"I met Steph through a team building session and was blown away by the accuracy with which she interpreted people and their situations. I appreciated her straightforwardness and easy engagement style. A few years later at a challenging time in my career I contacted Steph again for 121 coaching. Using tools in this chapter like Strengthscope, My Life So Far and The Values exercises, I was able to navigate my situation by creating focus on my natural strengths and values.

Thanks to Steph and the tools in this chapter I grew stronger in consciously leading from my values and strengths. I understood what professional environments are a good fit for me and how I can use my strengths to support and develop other people in the organization. I also found a position and a company that are more aligned to my strengths and values. I may never have found this role and company if it wasn't for the help Steph gave me."

BREGJE MEUWISSEN - Group Chief Human Resources Officer – Cint

**Without LEAPS
of imagination,
or dreaming, we
lose the excitement
of possibilities.
Dreaming, after all,
is a form of planning.**

———

Gloria Steinem
Journalist and Social-political activist

Chapter 3

Getting clear what I want
and why I want it

Chapter 3
Getting clear what I want and why I want it

WHAT STOPS US LIVING THE LIFE WE WANT?

Over the years I have seen three common reasons emerge around what stops my coaching clients living the life they want, or doing work they love. I mentioned these reasons in my introduction to this book.

1. They don't really know what they want
2. They don't believe they can get what they want
3. They don't know where to start or can't think clearly

These reasons often mean that my clients have given up thinking about taking a leap before they've even given it a chance. When actually all they need to do is to spend some productive thinking time working out what they want, why they want it, and how they can get it.

However, we can all get sucked into just reacting to life, and rarely spend focused time proactively and productively thinking about exactly what we want or why we want it, let alone making a plan for how we're going to get it.

We might mull over a few ideas in our head, but never really bring any clarity to those ideas because we shut them down almost as quickly as they arise.

The tools and techniques I'm going to share with you in this chapter will help you in a very practical way to overcome some of the mental barriers that have stopped you thinking about what you want.

There are tools in this chapter that will help you to **DREAM** and visualise, and tools that will help you to get **PRACTICAL** and organised about it all.

But before we get into the tools, let me explain a bit about the science behind why we find any sort of future thinking hard. Just to reassure you that it's often due to the limitations of our brains, that we don't do the things we really want to do, or really know we should do.

WHY THINKING ABOUT THE FUTURE IS HARD

There's a wealth of research in the field of neuroscience that demonstrates how hard it is for our brains to do future thinking.

Thinking about the future contains two elements that the brain finds hard to process, and therefore takes more energy to think about. The future is **1. Uncertain** and **2. Hard to control**.

Our brains find it difficult to deal with **uncertainty** because uncertainty is perceived in the brain as a threat. When the brain experiences a threat, the emotional reaction of fear will be triggered. So as soon as we start to think about the future, we can often go into an immediate state of worry and fear, and this stops us thinking clearly.

We can't think clearly when we experience fear and worry, because the part of the brain that helps us do all our rational and logical thinking (the prefrontal cortex) is prevented from functioning. This means we are physically unable to use the part of the brain that could help us to think rationally about the future. Our brain just can't do it. Chapter 4 goes into a bit more detail on the science behind how this all works.

Your brain also likes to feel in control. But of course there are so many factors that can affect how the future might turn out, that when you start to think about it, you don't feel fully able to determine, predict or know for sure what will happen. This perceived lack of control over the future then generates the same fear response in our brains as uncertainty.

So uncertainty, and a sense of not being in control, make future thinking hard to do because they trigger the fear response. The fear response then stops your rational brain from working, which in turn inhibits your ability to do any practical, proactive or productive thinking about the future.

The key here then is to find ways to help your brain cope with the uncertainty and lack of control that the future presents.

HOW TO HELP YOUR BRAIN THINK ABOUT THE FUTURE

Your brain needs some structure to help it think about the future, as well as some reassurance that you don't have to have everything figured out right now, or be completely certain about what will happen.

 Strive for clarity not certainty.

Bob Johansen
Author & Professional Futurist

So a good place to start is to focus on **gaining clarity of what you want**, and put on hold thinking about how you're going to get there.

Gaining clarity helps the brain feel back in control.

Give yourself permission to dream, and take away the pressure (for now) of having to know exactly what you're going to do to make it happen.

To gain clarity on what you want, I have included tools in this chapter that will help you to expand your thinking beyond what you think is possible, and in essence dream like a child around what you think would be amazing.

There are also some tools included here that will help you to fine tune your ideas and start to get really specific on what your ideal life would or could look and feel like.

These tools will give your brain the structure it needs to not get triggered into the fear response when thinking about the future. The tools will effectively help you to do more **productive thinking** about your ideas, rather than just letting them swirl aimlessly about in your head.

But let's ease gradually into this 'future thinking' by starting with the present, and what you already know about yourself.

WHAT ARE YOUR INTERESTS AND PASSIONS?

We all have interests and passions in certain topics and activities. These interests, passions and activities can hold clues to what we really want to do with our lives.

We often dismiss these passions and interests as just hobbies, that we could never create a career out of. For some of those passions and interests, that may well be true. But in my experience, most people jump to an immediate conclusion and dismiss their passions before they've given them any serious thought or even tried to incorporate them into their career.

Yet these are the things that get you out of bed in the morning. The thought of doing them enables you to make it through the week knowing you'll have the reward of your favourite hobby or pastime at the weekend.

These are also the things that you do willingly and not just for the money. You do these things because you enjoy them or because they bring meaning to your life. So imagine what it might feel like if you could get all that joy from doing them, and get paid!

Now, after completing the next few exercises, it might turn out that you are happy to keep these interests or activities as hobbies, and not make them part of your career, and that's ok. It means the exercises have given you clarity that you might not have achieved before. The key point here is that clarifying your passions can help you to see what might be missing in either your life at home or at work.

For example, you may be really interested in living sustainably and protecting the planet, so you passionately do everything you can in your personal life to live in a way that causes the least impact. However, you work for a company that has little interest in being sustainable. This is likely to cause a conflict inside of you as well as affect your motivation at work. But you might not have realised this until you spent productive thinking time identifying what's important to you.

So once you become clearer on what you're interested in, what you're passionate about, and even where you might want to make a difference in the world, this can help you to see where you could take small steps to getting more of those aspects into your life.

It's like making a check-list of all the things that matter to you, and then taking steps towards getting those things into your life (at work or at home).

There are four key categories that *Tool 7 - My passions and interests* asks you to look at. These are:

1. **Passions** - Issues and causes close to your heart
2. **Hobbies** - Activities you do in your spare time
3. **Interests** - Subjects or topics you love to investigate
4. **Making a difference** - The parts of life you feel strongly about making a difference in

Now you might find that your answers could fit into more than one of the above categories, or there might be a bit of repetition or crossover, that's ok. This exercise is not about trying to find different answers to fit all four categories. The questions in the exercise are just prompts to help stimulate your ideas, and different questions or categories will work better for different people.

There may also be different reasons behind why certain causes have become important to you, and so the different categories and questions are designed to help tap into those differences. For instance, events in your personal life or the life of someone close to you, may have had such an impact on you that you now spend your spare time volunteering at a charity helping support others going through the same experience.

Alternatively, there may be issues that you care about like global warming or gender equality, that have simply arisen out of a core interest or value of yours.

So have a look at the tool on the next page to explore this further.

Tool 7

MY PASSIONS AND INTERESTS

Look back at your **My life so far** timeline and write down any events or experiences that had an impact on you, which then resulted in you feeling strongly about an issue related to that event or experience.

What subjects do you tend to talk passionately about? Have a look back at your values to see if they inspire any passions.

What would your friends and family say you talk passionately about? (if you don't know, ask them).

Who do you follow on social media and why do you follow them?

What brands do you buy, or companies/organisations do you admire, and why?

What do you do in your free time? What do you make time to do? What would you do even if you weren't paid to do it?

You can now fill in the sections on your passions, hobbies and interests, and where you want to make a difference on p.83.

Once you've started identifying your passions and interests, it will then become easier to start to imagine what your ideal life might look like, and funnily enough *Tool 8 - My ideal life*, is the next tool for you to try out.

This tool is all about dreaming. It's about suspending reality for a moment, shutting up the 'yeah buts', and allowing yourself to imagine what your ideal life would or could look like.

Now with this exercise it might feel like you're not actually being that productive, but as Alan Oram once said to me:

Dreaming about possibilities could sound a bit airy fairy. Or it could be the start of something magical.

Alan Oram
Founder and Director at Alive with Ideas

So, just for a moment, I'd like you to imagine that anything is possible. You can go back to reality and the 'yeah buts' in a bit. In fact it's important that you do address the 'yeah buts', but not yet!

If I could wave a magic wand and tell you that all those 'yeah buts' won't be a problem and you could have everything you wanted in your ideal life... what would that life look like?

On the next page are six steps to help you set yourself up for this exercise. Then on the pages that follow, you'll find questions to help you describe what your *Ideal life* would look like.

The key here is to make this an entirely enjoyable activity.

Tool 8

MY IDEAL LIFE

SIX STEPS to making this an enjoyable activity

 **Choose a day** that you will start your *Ideal life* activity. Plan in 30 minutes.

 **Choose a space** that you would enjoy spending time in. This could be a certain room in your house, or a favourite cafe, or somewhere outside in nature.

 **Choose a drink** that you love, and grab your favourite snack.

 **Choose a notepad** or piece of paper you'd enjoy writing on, or maybe you like to brainstorm standing up with sticky notes, or just straight onto your laptop.

 **Remove distractions** by turning your phone off, and minimising any other possible external interruptions.

 **Give permission** to yourself to consider what would be amazing not just what you think is possible.

Tool 8

MY IDEAL LIFE

Answer the following questions, but remember to think about what would be **AMAZING** not what you think is **POSSIBLE**!

Thinking about My ideal life...

What specific things in my personal life would I like to do or try?

What would my ideal day/week look like?

How would I be spending my time? How would I divide my time up (e.g. time at home, time with family or friends, time at work, time on interests and hobbies)?

What sort of things would I like to be doing for work?

If I could work in any way that I wanted, how would that be? E.g. do I mainly work at home, or do I have an office? Do I travel to clients?

How much money would I be earning? How much do I want to earn a month or a year to maintain the sort of life I want to lead?

Tool 8

In your current or previous roles, what have you really loved doing? When were three times that you were really energised, or in flow and totally loving what you were doing? Write them below.

The times when I have been totally loving what I've been doing at work have been:

Why do I want a life like the one I've described here, what will it give me?

OK, SO WHAT'S NEXT?

How was that as an experience? Did you make it enjoyable? Did you allow yourself to dream for a bit? Did you get some clues as to what would make you happy in your ideal life? I hope you got a few insights, if not the complete picture!

However, I suspect you probably kept being interrupted by a voice in your head that said:

'Yeah but, this isn't real life is it?'
or *'Yeah but, it's impossible to get everything you want!'*
or *'Yeah but, isn't this a bit self-indulgent?'*

If you did get any of those 'yeah buts', or any variation on them, that's perfectly normal, we're not used to letting ourselves picture our ideal life. Make a note of the 'yeah buts' you had below, as we'll be tackling them in the next chapter.

My 'yeah buts' were:

Also, if part of you is feeling a bit guilty for spending so much time on yourself, I always like to think about the advice they give on a plane if problems occur - put your own oxygen mask on before helping others. By helping yourself first, you'll be in a much stronger position to help others.

 "Whoever is happy will make others happy too"

Anne Frank
Diarist

Tool 9

ME AT MY BEST

Use this page to pull together a summary of everything you've learned so far about you at your best!

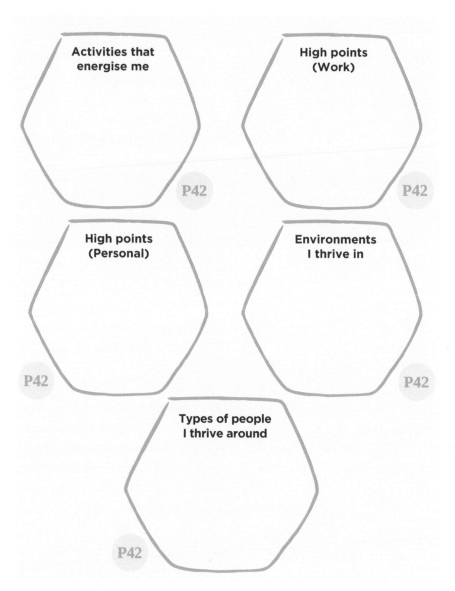

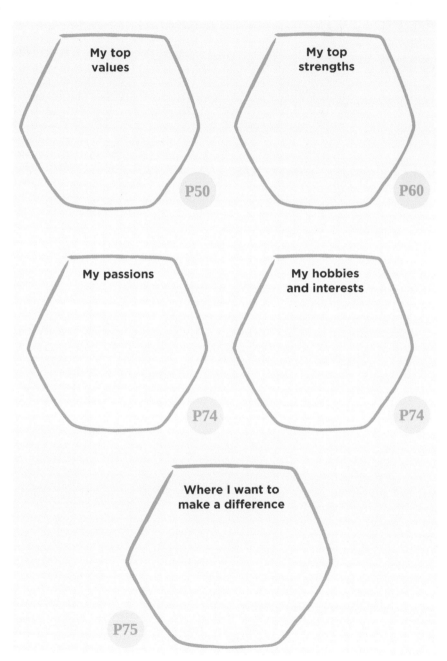

My top values

P50

My top strengths

P60

My passions

P74

My hobbies and interests

P74

Where I want to make a difference

P75

Making my plan

MY REFLECTIONS AND INSIGHTS

Make a note below of any reflections or insights you've had from reading Chapter 3.

Did anything particularly resonate with you?
How do you feel having read Chapter 3?

My reflections, insights, thoughts or feelings:

MY ACTIONS

Make a note below of any actions you would like to take as a result of the reflections and insights you captured after reading Chapter 3.

Actions I want to take:

Kind words from my clients about the tools and techniques in this chapter.

"*Having spent 20 years in the corporate world, I contacted Steph as I wasn't feeling the same drive, motivation and enthusiasm in this space that I had for so many years prior. Steph's tool 'My Ideal Life' spurred me on to follow my passions and dreams to move away from the '9 to 5', start my own business and pursue those ambitions that aligned with my purpose. I've now successfully started my own business ventures and am living a life that has rekindled that drive, motivation and enthusiasm that I had previously lost.*"

BIRAJ NAKARJA - Non-Executive Director & Coach

"*The exercises in this chapter gave me far more confidence and clarity about what I wanted next for both myself and my business. The best thing about working with Steph is her belief that you can't separate your professional life from your personal life. Working with Steph feels like you're having coffee with a friend, with the added bonus of coming away with a huge amount of insight and understanding.*"

HELEN DEVERELL - Internal Communications Consultant

"Using many of the tools and techniques in this chapter, Steph helped me realise that my personality was not suited to corporate life. She coached me through the transition from corporate board member to entrepreneur. I now get to be at my best every day, running a multi-million pound technology company, and enjoying seeing something flourish and grow."

RICHARD ALEXANDER - Entrepreneur and Business Investor

Learn to travel comfortably with your FEAR, if not, you'll never **do anything interesting.**

———

Elizabeth Gilbert
Author

Chapter 4

Overcoming my '...Yeah buts'

Chapter 4
Overcoming my '...Yeah buts'

ADDRESSING YOUR '...YEAH BUTS'

In the first chapter I introduced what I believe are the real reasons why you're getting stuck and not taking the leap you want to take. These were:

THE REAL REASONS YOU'RE STUCK:

- You **underestimate** the power of your **NATURAL STRENGTHS** and the unique value you **already** offer

- You've not spent **PRODUCTIVE THINKING** time working out what you want and what's important to you

- Your emotions (**fear and worry mainly**) are clouding your thinking and judgement.

In chapter 2 I gave you some tools to overcome the first reason by helping you to understand, value and appreciate your unique natural strengths and what you already offer the world. In chapter 3, I gave you some tools to help you to address the second reason by putting aside your "yeah buts" and allowing yourself to do some productive thinking about what you want in your ideal life and why you want it.

In this chapter, I am going to focus on overcoming the third reason by helping you to understand and manage the emotions that are getting in your way of leaping. Managing your emotions better will enable you to tackle those "yeah buts" that are currently stopping you from taking a leap.

HOW DO EMOTIONS STOP US FROM LEAPING?

Our emotions drive our behaviour, in everything we do and every decision we make, so they will have a huge impact on whether you take the leap you want to take. It's surprising that something that can so fundamentally impact the quality of our day to day lives was completely left off the school syllabus.

...ok so what's the tally now on what's been left off the school syllabus that could have helped us?

Not understanding our emotions can lead us to believing that there's not much we can do about them. This leaves us feeling stuck, and at the mercy of any emotion that shows up in us.

Left off the school syllabus

✓ *Understanding our natural strengths and what makes us unique*

✓ *Figuring out what we want to do with our lives*

✓ *Understanding our emotions and how to manage them*

#justsaying

YOU ARE IN CONTROL OF YOUR EMOTIONS

You may believe that you're not in control of how you feel, but the good news is that you are more in control of your emotions than you might think.

There is always something you can do to manage or regulate your emotions, especially if you understand the science behind emotions, as well as how and why they show up in you.

Every person experiences and expresses emotions. But the extent to which they show up and are expressed can vary from person to person. Some people feel emotions more deeply than others, and some people express them more outwardly than others. Every person is different. So, when going through this chapter it is important not to compare yourself to others, but to get really clear on how emotions show up and express themselves in you.

WHY DO WE HAVE EMOTIONS?

Emotions are natural, normal responses to the events that happen in our lives. The purpose of emotions is to help us to survive, that is why they fundamentally drive our behaviour. Emotions get triggered rapidly and automatically by situations, people, and even thoughts; and can appear as if from out of nowhere, that's why it can feel like they are not in our control.

As human beings, we experience a range of emotions that psychologists have categorised into nine emotion families. The research to fully understand these families is ongoing.

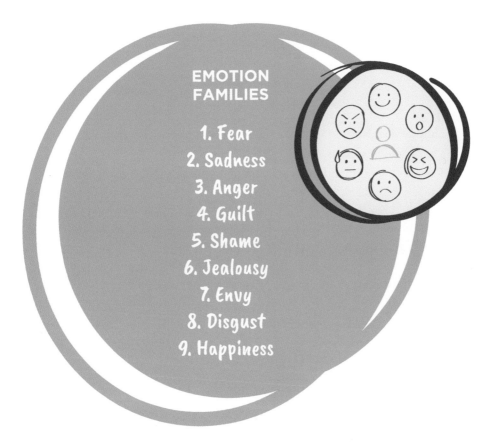

EMOTION
FAMILIES

1. Fear
2. Sadness
3. Anger
4. Guilt
5. Shame
6. Jealousy
7. Envy
8. Disgust
9. Happiness

Current research has found that each of the nine emotion families contain emotions that can be felt at different intensities. This accounts for the many variations of feelings we experience, and therefore the many different words we have within each emotion family.

For example, the variations of feelings in the fear family can range from mild concern, through to worry, anxiety and terror.

You can see this on the fear spectrum below:

All emotions share three core qualities:

1. They have a purpose for showing up in us
2. They initiate an urge to act
3. They prepare our bodies to take action to help us survive

Understanding the purpose of each emotion family, what action it stimulates us to want to take, and how that emotion shows up in our bodies, can be a great first step into helping you to manage and take control of that emotion.

The emotions that can most often affect whether you leap or not will tend to be those within the emotion family of fear, and so that is the only emotion family that I'll focus on in this book. However, if you would like to know more about the other emotions, please get in touch, my contact details are at the end of this book (p.144).

THE SCIENCE OF HOW FEAR STOPS YOU LEAPING

There are two key parts of our brain that are relevant to how fear, and in fact all emotions affect us.

1. The limbic system – this is the part of the brain that processes our emotions. It often operates below our conscious awareness and is hyper sensitive and hyper vigilant, looking out for events, experiences and people who might threaten our survival and well-being. This is the oldest part of our brain from an evolutionary perspective.

2. The prefrontal cortex – this is the part of our brain where we do our more logical and rational thinking. The prefrontal cortex is involved in slower and more conscious processes, and from an evolutionary perspective, is the newest part of our brain.

You could think of the limbic system as our emotional part of the brain, and the prefrontal cortex as the logical part of our brain.

Your brain...

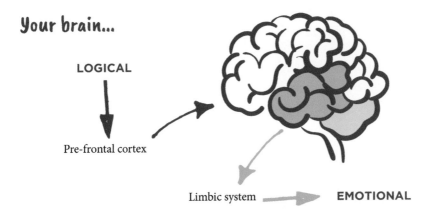

Our brain's main purpose is to help us to survive; so if it feels like we are in danger, our limbic system will create an emotional reaction of FEAR. This emotion will then prepare our body to be able to fight or run away, (known as the fight, flight or freeze response). This is a quick and automatic response in our limbic system and is designed to protect us. Ultimately our brain wants to minimise danger and maximise safety.

So for example, if you imagine back in our prehistoric days, we were literally trying to physically survive. One of the biggest threats to our survival were the predators like sabre tooth tigers. So if we came face to face with one, our limbic system would kick into action, tell us there's a threat and prepare our bodies to run away. Again, this was all going on under our conscious awareness, it happens so quickly and automatically.

So why is this relevant to us today? There's no sabre tooth tigers lurking on our streets... *(well maybe a few in our offices).*

This is relevant today, because our brain cannot tell if a threat is real in the form of a sabre tooth tiger, or perceived in the form of an unreasonable boss, unending to do list, demanding family, or the uncertainty of taking a leap in our career.

So if we perceive an event to be threatening, the fear response will kick in.

It's interesting to note here that **perceived financial loss** has been found to **register in the same part of the brain as mortal danger.** So it's no wonder we can be afraid to take a leap.

The other important factor here is that when the limbic system is aroused, i.e. when we feel any emotion, and particularly any emotion in the fear family, our prefrontal cortex is physically unable to work. The limbic system literally stops the prefrontal cortex from working, because there is a need for a rapid response, and the prefrontal cortex will slow things down.

You can see this in the two triangles on the next page. As the limbic system triangle gets bigger, the prefrontal cortex triangle gets smaller.

This is why we might not be able to think straight when we try to do our productive thinking about what we want, because the part of the brain that helps us to think rationally has been prevented from working.

So it's important to deal with the fear, so you can get the prefontal cortex working again.

Your brain's purpose is to help you to survive

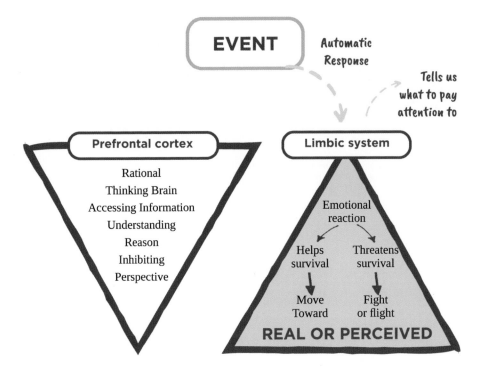

Over arousal of the limbic system reduces the ability
of the pre frontal cortex to function

THE PROBLEM WITH SUPPRESSING EMOTIONS

It's also important to note here that even if you suppress any feelings of fear, worry or concern, and pretend they aren't there, the physiological response will still be going on in your body. So the limbic system will still be shutting down the prefrontal cortex. This means that you're not doing yourself any favours by ignoring the feeling, you need to deal with it before you can start to get your rational brain back in the game.

HOW TO OVERCOME A FEAR OF LEAPING

To begin to manage or regulate the impact an emotion like fear is having on you, you need to notice the fear as soon as it shows up in you. You then need to accept it is there, which is not always easy to do. But accepting that the emotion is there is crucial if you want to address and manage the impact that the emotion is having on you. The signs that you are feeling any emotion often show up in your thoughts.

So to specifically overcome fears of leaping, let's focus in on the most common thoughts my clients experience when considering taking a leap. These thoughts are the signs that they have been feeling some form of fear, and are often expressed as 'YEAH BUTS'.

COMMON THOUGHTS THAT STOP PEOPLE LEAPING

YEAH BUT what if I can't pay the mortgage?

YEAH BUT what if I can't do it or make it work?

YEAH BUT what if I don't get any clients?

YEAH BUT what will people think of me if this fails?

YEAH BUT what if I don't fit in anymore?

YEAH BUT it's selfish/self-indulgent for me to do this

Through years of working with my clients who want to take a leap, I have realised that these common thoughts fall into one of two categories of more deeply held fears, these are:

1. A fear of failing
2. A fear of being rejected

There is also the fear of success. Yes really, that does exist. But when you unpick what someone is ultimately afraid of if they succeed, it turns out they are afraid of being rejected. People who fear succeeding, experience thoughts like -*What if I no longer fit in. What if I can't connect with my friends and family, or they can't connect with me?*

Out of the two main categories of fear, by far the greatest fear that I see people having is - **the FEAR OF FAILURE!** So let's explore how to manage that.

OVERCOMING THE FEAR OF FAILURE

When someone says *"yeah but what if I fail?"* I ask them:

What do you mean by fail? What are you picturing?

I ask this question because the word **'failure' is a really loaded and unhelpful word.**

But we almost carelessly, thoughtlessly and unconsciously chuck the word 'failure' around and don't really explore what we mean by it. It just fuels an emotional response of fear, and so we don't dare to go near it.

But technically, it is only ever failure if there is just one finite possible way of something being done, and if you only get one chance at achieving it within a specific and defined timeframe.

Anything else really isn't failure.

Let's say your goal is to run the 100 metres in under 9.5 seconds at the next Olympics, and it's your last chance to do it. The big day arrives, but you run the distance in 9.6 seconds. Then yes you've failed. Your goal was so specific and timebound, and you only had one opportunity to do it.

However, in most situations you will always have another opportunity. As such, it feels more appropriate (and rational) to apply Stanford University Psychology Professor Dr Carol Dweck's ideas about holding a growth mindset when responding to your fear of failing.

Arguably two of the greatest competitors in their sports, Michael Jordan and Serena Williams, articulated beautifully what holding a growth mindset looks like when they respectively said:

I've missed more than 9,000 shots in my career. I've lost almost 300 games. Twenty-six times, I've been trusted to take the game winning shot and missed. I've failed over and over and over again in my life. And that is why I succeed.

Micheal Jordan
Former Professional Basketball Player

I don't like to lose - at anything - yet I've grown most not from victories, but from my setbacks.

Serena Williams
Former Professional Tennis Player

EXPLORING HOW A GROWTH MINDSET CAN HELP

Here's a couple of questions for you. On questions 1-3, draw a circle around the number that best matches how much you agree or disagree with these statements. On question 4, answer a or b. There are no right or wrong answers.

1. I am a certain kind of person and there is not much that can be done to really change that.

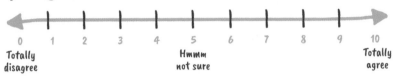

2. I can learn new things, but I can't really change my abilities.

3. I can always change how intelligent I am.

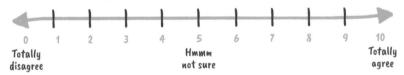

4. When faced with a problem that feels too hard to solve, I think that:
   (circle the answer you are most likely to think)
   a. I'm just not smart enough to solve it.
   b. I just haven't solved it yet.

Keep a note of your answers, as we will return to them later. For now, let me tell you more about the growth mindset approach.

Dr Carol Dweck completed decades of research into what influences our ability to succeed. It's an interesting use of the word 'ability' here, because her research seems to show, over and over again, that it's not your ability that determines your success, but moreover **your beliefs about your ability**.

Her studies found that those who have what she calls **a growth mindset** as opposed to **a fixed mindset** were much more likely to improve their abilities in the tasks they were given. Particularly in those tasks they found challenging.

She found that our abilities are not fixed, but that they can in fact be developed, **especially if you BELIEVE they can be developed**.

Seems like Lewis Carroll knew this too!

> **Alice: "This is impossible"**
> **Mad Hatter: "Only if you believe it is"**
> Lewis Carroll

In her TED talk, Dr Carol Dweck describes a lovely example of a school that instead of giving 'fail' as a grade, gives a **Not Yet** grade. The knock on effect of this was that the children who were schooled in this environment went on to achieve higher grades than those who weren't.

The NOT YET grade helped the school children believe that what they were trying to achieve was within their reach, and so they kept trying. The more they tried, the more their abilities improved.

What's brilliant and amazing about this mindset is that **it puts failure in a whole new light.**

For those with a growth mindset, failure is a concept they don't even recognise. Not succeeding in a task is seen as an opportunity to learn, not a finite reflection of their ability to succeed or fail.

Not being able to solve something, to these crazy growth mindsetter type folk, is actually fun and rewarding.

REALLY? I hear you ask in utter disbelief!

It's true, well Dweck's research certainly seems to indicate the truth of it. Also, if you look at most of the people who succeed in whatever venture, industry or issue they choose to engage with, they pretty much have the same quality: **...they embrace failure and just keep trying.**

To name just a few: JK Rowling, Chris Evans, Richard Branson, Jessica Ennis Hill, Mo Farah, Walt Disney, Sir James Dyson, Oprah Winfrey, Bill Gates, Katy Perry, Jim Carey, Fred Astaire, Vincent Van Gogh, Theodor Seuss Giesel (i.e. Dr. Seuss), Vera Wang, Elvis Presley, Stravinsky, The Beatles, Hillary Devey, Arianna Huffington, Christine Lagarde.

JK Rowling for example, was a single mother, near enough broke, divorced, depressed and had rejections from the 12 major publishers before Harry Potter was published by Bloomsbury.

Walt Disney was fired by the Editor of the Kansas City Star because they said "he lacked imagination", and his first film studio Laugh-O-Gram films went bankrupt.

When they were just starting out, The Beatles were told by a recording company, that "we don't like your sound, and guitar music is on the way out."

For 12 years, Vera Wang trained to be an olympic figure skater, but failed to make it to the Olympics. She changed careers and worked at Vogue aiming to become Editor in Chief, but failed again. It was not until she was 40, that she designed her own wedding dress and later became one of the world's most successful fashion designers.

People with a growth mindset believe that it is their effort and attitude, not their abilities that determine their success!

Someone with a growth mindset values what they are learning as much, if not more, than their intended outcome. They are therefore more likely to take on challenges that look hard. Whereas those with a fixed mindset are more likely to avoid those same challenges. This last point has HUGE implications for the sorts of goals you set yourself, especially when concerned with the type of life and career you want.

HOW YOUR MINDSET AFFECTS THE GOALS YOU SET

If you have a fixed mindset it is very likely that you are not going to set goals that you feel are beyond your reach, even if they are things you want to do.

 For most of us, the problem isn't that we aim too high and fail, the problem is we aim too low and succeed!

Sir Ken Robinson

Author, Speaker & Government Advisor

But, with a growth mindset you are far more likely to set those stretching goals, as you believe your current abilities are capable of growth.

So let's go back to your scores on the four questions I asked you. By now I suspect you have worked out whether you have a growth or fixed mindset. But here's what the answers mean.

It is likely that you have a growth mindset the more you disagreed with statements one and two, agreed with statement three and answered b in question four. The good news here though, is that no matter whether your answers revealed that you currently have a growth or a fixed mindset, your mindset can change and flex, depending on the situation and over time. Dr Carol Dweck's research shows that it is possible to develop a growth mindset if you want to.

So when it comes to addressing the fear of failure, I think it is fair to say that in most situations, if something doesn't go to plan, it's quite likely that you will have another chance to make it work. So it won't technically be a failure. The real issue here is more about how many times you're willing and able to try. Adopting a growth mindset can help support you to keep trying.

PRACTICAL ACTIONS TO OVERCOME YOUR FEARS

As well as adopting a growth mindset, there are also some practical actions you can take to overcome any specific thoughts that are preventing you from taking a leap.

Earlier I highlighted the most common thoughts that stop people leaping, and categorised these thoughts into two types of fears: a fear of failure and a fear of rejection. Here's a quick reminder of the common thoughts and how they fit into the two types of fear.

Type of fear	Thoughts you're likely to have if this fear is stopping you leap
Fear of Failure	What if I can't pay the mortgage? What if I can't get any clients? What if I can't do it/make it work?
Fear of Rejection	What will people think of me if this fails? What if I don't fit in anymore? It's selfish/self-indulgent for me to do this.

One of the best ways to overcome the thoughts that stop us from leaping, is to take some sort of action or carry out experiments to challenge those thoughts.

In the next few pages you will find practical tips and actions you can take to address or challenge these common thoughts and the fears that sit behind them.

You can't really stop a thought from popping into your head, but whether it takes root, is weeded out, or gets bonsai-ed into a more desirable, lasting shape, depends on you.

Dr Erin Olivio PHD
Clinical Psychologist, Author & Ass. Clinical Professor of Medical Psychology

WHAT IF I CAN'T PAY THE MORTGAGE?

This thought usually comes from an assumption that a leap will mean you have to take either a permanent, or a temporary cut in income or salary.

Now that may well be true. But are you sure?

Is this just an assumption that you've not properly investigated? Have you looked into this in every detail? If you've not fully explored this, then a good first step would be to talk to people who are already doing what you want to be doing, to see what the reality is.

However, if you know for sure, or there is a real risk that you will need to take a cut in income, then have a look at the following actions.

 Actions

> **Actions to take**
>
> - Work out how much money you need a month to cover your bills and outgoings.
>
> - Identify how long you think it will take to make your leap work whilst on a lower income, or on no income (how many weeks, months or years?)
>
> - Plan to save that amount of money to cover your outgoings until your leap brings in enough money, or, identify outgoings that could be reduced.

These actions will help you build a financial safety net to help support you to leap. They may also highlight how far away or even how close you are to being able to leap. Either way they should give you a tangible plan and help to reduce the worry over being able to pay the mortgage.

WHAT IF I CAN'T/DON'T GET ANY CLIENTS?

This is the most common thought I see people have who want to leave corporate life and set up a business. It is an absolutely warranted thought if you have never had to find clients or customers before.

However, it doesn't have to be something to be afraid of. It can be converted into a question, i.e. How do I go about getting clients?

So instead of worrying about whether you can get clients or not, recognise that it's not something you've done before, but it is something you can learn how to do. There are people out there like you, who once didn't know how to get clients, but are now managing to attract all the clients they need.

 Actions

> **Actions to take**
>
> • Talk to people who are already running a business about how they get clients. (I suspect most will say they get them through word of mouth and through their network.)
>
> • Look at your existing network and focus on nurturing those relationships by getting back in touch with people and letting them know what you're thinking of doing.
>
> • If you don't have a relevant or big enough network, start to build one.

These actions will help you to learn and apply the techniques of the people who are already doing what you want to be doing. It might feel daunting to contact people you haven't spoken to for a long time, however most people are usually very happy to reconnect and understand how we can all get absorbed into our own lives and not keep in touch with people as much as we'd like.

WHAT IF I CAN'T DO IT OR MAKE IT WORK?

This thought usually comes from self-doubt, and an assumption that you don't believe you are good enough, experienced enough, qualified enough or credible enough to make this work.

I suspect that if you have this thought, it's likely that you've **only** been focusing on what you don't have, instead of fully exploring what you've already got that can help you.

 Actions

> ### Actions to take
>
> - Make a list of all the experiences, skills, strengths, qualities, contacts, knowledge, qualifications and resources you think you might need to make your leap work.
>
> - Put a tick against all the experiences, skills, strengths, qualities, contacts, knowledge, qualifications and resources you already have.
>
> - Then identify which experiences, skills, strengths, qualities, contacts, knowledge, qualifications and resources are the most important to have right now, and if you don't have them, then make a plan to get them.

These actions will help you to uncover what you already have that will enable you to make the leap happen, as well as what the priority gaps are that need filling before you leap.

WHAT WILL PEOPLE THINK OF ME IF THIS FAILS?

When someone says 'what will people think of me' I've found that on closer inspection what they mean is - what will a few key people in my life think of me. These are usually people who's thoughts and advice someone places a disproportionate amount of importance on. Whether that's a boss, a friend, a partner, parent or influential relative.

These people are usually just trying to keep you safe, and their thoughts tend to be more of a reflection of themselves, than of you.

Some of these people may also make remarks based on their own agendas. For example, a boss who tells you to stay a bit longer to get more experience, but who really doesn't want you to go. Or a parent who says 'you've got to be sensible', but who can't bear to see you hurt and afraid, or that you may not need them anymore.

  Actions

> **Actions to take**
>
> • Ask yourself about who you are referring to when you say 'people'?
>
> • Decide if you really want to listen to them.
>
> • Explore whether they really know what you need, want or are capable of doing?

This action will help you to identify who precisely you are worried about, and whether you want to be influenced by them.

WHAT IF I DON'T FIT IN ANY MORE?

This thought usually comes from a fear of success, or a fear that by following a path towards what you want, you will be doing something very different to the people around you.

So you fear that your friends and family won't understand you, won't support you or won't be able to connect with you, (or you with them) anymore.

 Actions

Actions to take

- This is about recognising that you are growing in a different direction to some of your friends and family. That's ok. It might mean that you need to stop listening to their advice on this matter, or that you need to redefine the relationship in terms of what you need from each other.

- It is also a sign that now is a good time to find an additional support network of people who are more aligned to how you want to live.

- So start to make contact with people who are already doing what you want to be doing and start to hang out more with people who are your supporters and cheerleaders.

These actions will help you to stay connected to your current friends and family, but just re-define the relationships, as well as help you to see that there are others out there who can help and who want to support you.

IT'S SELFISH/SELF INDULGENT FOR ME TO DO THIS

This thought usually comes from a belief that everyone else's needs are more important than your own.

You are also likely to be in a life situation where you have a lot of caring responsibilities, either you are bringing up children, or you are caring for an elderly or sick relative.

It's also likely with this thought, that you have made an assumption that you can't possibly have both the career you want and look after those who are dependent on you.

 Actions

Actions to take

• Get clear what you really want to do, and what steps you need to take to make it happen.

• Identify if you could do a smaller version of what you want to do (for now), or if there are any small steps you can start to take.

• Speak to your family, friends, partner and dependents (where appropriate) about what you'd like to do, and work together to help make it happen, so that everyone's needs are met.

These actions will help you to challenge any assumptions you've made about what you can and can't do, and enlist the support of those around you.

THIS PROCESS MAY AFFECT YOUR RELATIONSHIPS

Moving towards a dream that is important to you, and moving closer towards who you really are and what you really want, can at times be very challenging when it comes to your relationships with family and friends.

This is because the process of addressing your '...Yeah Buts' can highlight where you've not been fully yourself, where you've suppressed your own needs or values, or where you've been behaving in ways to appease someone else or to fit in, rather than in ways that support you.

So don't be surprised if this process brings up some discomfort as you question some of your relationships. You might start getting cross at your family for appearing to hold you back, or sad that your friends don't seem to understand you. This is all a natural part of the process.

But remember, you've been doing all this work in the background, and so you may have to spend some time updating your family and friends on what you're discovering. You don't have to suddenly ditch everyone in your current life, but you may need to re-define your relationship with them. I would also suggest you make it a priority to build a network of people who are your greatest supporters, and who do understand you. As the actor, director and philanthropist André De Shields says:

 Surround yourself with people whose eyes light up when they see you coming.

André De Shields
Actor, Director & Philanthropist

A GENERAL TIP ON OVERCOMING FEARS

The technique I've just taken you through to explore and challenge your thoughts about leaping, is a technique that comes from Cognitive Behaviour Therapy (CBT), and has been very effective for many of my clients.

One of the guiding principles of CBT is that our reactions (and therefore our feelings, like worry and fear) are not caused by the events that happen in our lives. Our reactions are caused by our **thoughts about** those events.

EVENT   **THOUGHT**   **REACTION**

So if you have any of the common thoughts listed on the previous pages, remember - **those are just thoughts!** They might not be reality. However, they will be generating a feeling of fear or worry which will prevent you from moving forward or trying to think through an idea.

CBT is also based on the principle that our thoughts, feelings and behaviours are so intrinsically linked, that if you change one of them, you can change the other two.

So a great technique here is to try to **change your thoughts.**
You can change your thoughts by **changing where you focus.**
This in turn will help to change **how you feel.**

Changing how you feel won't take the risk away that you might not be able to pay the mortgage, but it will help to click your prefrontal cortex back into action so you can think more clearly about your leap. It's not about fooling yourself here, it's about managing the emotion that is getting in your way of thinking rationally about your ideas.

Watch your thoughts, they become your words

Watch your words, they become your actions

Watch your actions, they become your habits

Watch your habits, they become your character

Watch your character, it becomes your destiny

Lao Tzu
Philosopher
and fouder of Taoism

Here are two ways you can challenge and change your focus, which should help you change your thoughts, and therefore change how you feel:

1. Ask focus shifting questions
2. Focus on regret not fear

HERE ARE SOME FOCUS SHIFTING QUESTIONS:

- What am I afraid of happening if I don't take the leap?

- If I don't do this, what will happen?

- If I stay here, how much worse am I/is it going to get?

- What will others think of me if I don't even try?

- What will I think of myself if I don't even try?

One of my clients asked herself the second question - "If I don't do this, what will happen?", this is what she said in response:

If I don't do this I'll end up in this same job with these same people who are talking the same BS for the rest of my life!

I'll stay stuck!

I will never be true to myself.

My passion will never be shared.

I'll be jealous that others did it and I didn't.

I'll be annoyed at myself.

I'll end up like my Dad and I really don't want that.

I'll regret a lost opportunity.

FOCUS ON REGRET NOT FEAR

Dan Pink, author of the book The Power of Regret, carried out extensive research into the feeling of regret, why we have regret, what sort of regrets we have, and how having regrets helps us live better lives.

One of the biggest findings that Dan Pink identified from his research is that as we get older:

We regret what we DIDN'T DO, more than what we did!

So rather than focusing on the fear about the future that you have right now, change your focus to the feeling of regret that you might feel in the future as you look back.

There's a fairly well-known exercise called the Rocking Chair exercise, where you picture yourself as an old person, near the end of your life, looking back over the life you've lived.

You then ask your rocking chair self, what regrets do you have?

This can be a powerful exercise to help you to identify what's most important to you, and therefore whether taking your leap is the right or best thing to do.

When you do this exercise, you may well find that it's more important to you to have certainty and stability, and that the leap isn't as important to you as some of the other aspects of your life right now.

On the other hand, the exercise may highlight how you'd rather take the risk and leap, than be left forever wondering what might have happened.

I'm not a failure because I didn't succeed, I'm a failure because I didn't try.

Kev from Netflix series Derek
by Ricky Gervais

Making my plan

MY REFLECTIONS AND INSIGHTS

Make a note below of any reflections or insights you've had from reading Chapter 4.

Did anything particularly resonate with you?
How do you feel having read Chapter 4?

My reflections, insights, thoughts or feelings:

MY ACTIONS

Make a note below of any actions you would like to take as a result of the reflections and insights you captured after reading Chapter 4.

Actions I want to take

The following quotes are
from three of my clients who had
an array of 'yeah buts...'.

Sometimes their 'yeah buts...'
were related to whether they felt
they were experienced, qualified
or smart enough.

Other times their 'yeah buts...'
were related to what they felt they
should or shouldn't be doing.

Kind words from my clients about the tools and techniques in this chapter.

"Steph has played a major part in my professional development right from the 121 coaching she gave me in my corporate life, to then helping me launch my business. The techniques in this chapter have helped me to grow in confidence, build my resilience and have been pivotal in my journey to transform into the best version of me."

SARAH MAKINDE - Freelance Chartered Psychologist

"I owe Steph a huge amount for the belief I now have in myself, what this has done for me in my career and how it has also helped all the people that work for me or with me. Life changing is the simplest way of summarising how the techniques in this chapter helped me as well as my overall experience of coaching with Steph."

GARY LOMAS - Sales Director - Onnec Group

"Coaching with Steph was invaluable in my corporate career by building my confidence to be myself at work. Largely thanks to the results of the exercises in this chapter, several months later I had the confidence to start my own company. The value of Steph's approach is not just in the short term results it brings; for me it has had a much longer term positive impact."

DAN ADLER - Senior Director Blue Yonder Strategic Transformation Consulting

**Great things are
not done by impulse,
but by a series
of** small things
brought together.

Vincent Van Gogh
Artist

Chapter 5

Creating a plan I can stick to

Chapter 5
Creating a plan I can stick to

MAKING YOUR LEAP HAPPEN

This last chapter is all about helping you to form your plan around what you're going to do to make your leap happen. Now, having gone through the previous chapters and exercises, you may have realised that you actually don't want or need to take the leap you thought you did, but instead you want to make other sorts of changes in your life.

So, whether you want to take a leap or whether you simply want to make some changes, having a plan made up of small, manageable steps over a period of time, can help break down what might at first feel like an overwhelming or impossibly enormous task.

This chapter is all about creating a practical yet exciting plan, that you can easily incorporate into your current life to help get you to where you want to go. You don't have to suddenly make everything happen all at once. But small steps taken every day will help build momentum, and before you know it, you'll be making that last step that takes you into the life you've designed.

Slowly is the fastest way to get to where you want to be.

André De Shields
Actor, Director & Philanthropist

On the next page you'll find some guidelines on how to pull your plan together. This includes creating a summary of actions you want to take, as well as an analysis of how likely you are to take them.

When questioning the likelihood of completing each action, it's really important to be honest with yourself, because the aim here is to **create a plan you feel you can stick to.**

Tool 10

CREATING A PLAN I CAN STICK TO

To create a plan that you will be able to stick to, firstly look back at the actions you have recorded on the Making my plan pages of this book.

Then in the table on the opposite page, make a summary of the most important actions you would like to take.

You can also add further actions, (that you may not have recorded in this book yet), on another table on the page after next (p.128).

Then for each action on both tables, answer the following question (this can be found in the second column of the table):

On a scale of 1-10 how likely is it that I will take this action?

With:

1 being **'highly unlikely'**, and
10 being **'nothing will stop me'**.

When you answer this question: **Be completely honest!**

The score you give may provide clues as to what could be stopping you take each action.

It might feel a little uncomfortable to own up to what could stop you taking an action. But being truthful with yourself will give you a chance to pre-empt and overcome any possible barriers you may have to taking those actions.

A SUMMARY OF MY MOST IMPORTANT ACTIONS

Action I would like to take	How likely is it that I will take this action? 1-10

Tool 10

ADDITIONAL ACTIONS I WOULD LIKE TO TAKE

Action I would like to take	How likely is it that I will take this action? 1-10

MY ACTIONS

For each of your actions, ask yourself two further questions:

1. What needs to happen to make the likelihood of completing this action closer to a 10?
2. What support do I need to help me get closer to a 10?

Make some notes below about what you need in order to increase the likelihood of taking these actions:

Tool 11

REVIEWING MY OBJECTIVES

Finally in this exercise, look back at the objectives you wanted to achieve by reading this book (see p.22). List them below.

Give each objective a score out of 10 in terms of how close you felt you were to achieving that objective BEFORE reading this book. With 1 being 'nowhere near', and 10 being 'totally smashing it'. Then rate how close you feel you are to achieving each objective AFTER reading this book. On the same scale.

Objective	Before 1-10	After 1-10

So what do you notice about your scores? Have they increased, decreased, or stayed the same? What work is still left to do?

For each of your objectives that you scored less than 10 on in the AFTER column, answer the following question:

What needs to happen, or what support do I need, to move this closer to a 10?

Make some notes below about what you need in order to move the achievement of your objectives closer to a 10:

BONUS TOOL

PROS & CONS +

I hope those last few tools have helped you to form a plan you can stick to!

Before ending this book, I wanted to add a bonus tool for you, as there is a situation that we haven't yet discussed that can affect whether someone leaps or not.

This is the situation when you have lots of ideas about what you could do, but don't know which way to go.

Having lots of ideas is great, but it can also pose a barrier to getting started. Sadly, all too often I see my clients doing nothing on any of their ideas because it all feels too overwhelming. So, I adapted a well-known decision making technique to help.

The technique is to write a pros and cons list on each idea, but also to think about how excited you are about each idea. This exercise can help you get a lot clearer on what your heart says you would like to do, as well as what your head says.

On the opposite page is a table where you can record the pros, the cons, and how excited you are about each idea.

In the pros column it's important to include all the skills, knowledge, resources and experience you already have to make each idea work. In the cons, it's important to include all the skills, knowledge, resources and experience that you feel you need.

By the end of this exercise you should be able to narrow down your ideas to the top one to three, and then make a plan to start to explore each of them further.

For each idea, write down all the pros and cons, as well as how excited you are about it

MY IDEAS (Include a brief description)	PROs (Motivations) (Including what I already have to help me with this)	CONs (Challenges) (Including what I need to help me with this)	How EXCITED am I? 1 = Not excited at all 10 = Really excited

BONUS TOOL

PROS & CONS +

Once you've identified your top three ideas, the next stage is to validate each of those ideas. It's important to validate your ideas because the reality doesn't always stack up to the dream.

For instance, Mark, a good friend of mine, told me that when he was younger he dreamt of being a lawyer. He wanted to become a lawyer because he had strong values in justice and fairness and wanted to make a difference in what he saw was an unfair and unjust world. The problem was that when he then did some work experience in a law firm, he realised that working in law was not what he thought it would be. He told me:

"It was not so much about justice, but more about making money in stuffy and hierarchical companies and legal systems with mind numbingly dull archaic detail."

His dream was not reality, the work wasn't enjoyable and the culture conflicted with his values and the way he liked to work. So, finding a way to validate your ideas is a good activity to add to your plan.

This might include chatting to people who are already doing what you would like to be doing, or volunteering in the job or industry you're interested in.

Mark is now working for a wonderful company whose mission is more aligned to his values. His story is an example of someone who has been clear what his values are, and has experimented with how to live by those values in how he works and who he works for.

On the opposite page you will find space to make some notes on how you might be able to validate each of your top three ideas.

NAME OF IDEA 1 ....

I could validate this idea by:

NAME OF IDEA 2 ....

I could validate this idea by:

NAME OF IDEA 3 ....

I could validate this idea by:

Kind words from my clients about the tools and techniques in this chapter.

"The Pro and Cons+ exercise helped me to get out of my head and onto paper the thoughts and ideas that had become a fog and a hindrance to me. Working through this exercise enabled me to see my options clearer with a more defined priority list of preferences. This exercise has helped me give clarity to a range of hypothetical ideas that were becoming too consuming for me to process and as a result stopping me move forward with conviction in my career."

DAVID STANLEY - Projects Director, Alive with Ideas

"Steph was able to understand my professional & personal drive, passion and desires very quickly and helped me establish my USP not only as a legal professional but also as a business person and a human.

Using the tools in this chapter we worked on short and long term goals in our sessions and I was held to account - if I wanted to achieve my outcomes I had to own my journey and could not be lazy or rely on anyone else. I still continue to utilise the plan and hold myself to account and can hear Steph's voice in my head.

I have used a few coaches over the years, but Steph by far has the most holistic and down to earth approach to coaching - you are not pigeon holed, you can explore both personal and professional development as at the end of the day we are all human and operate in the personal and business world simultaneously. The clarity and the options that I have before me have never been so clear."

BITESH SOLANKY - Director of Legal at Emeria UK

**Life is what happens
while you're busy
making other plans.**

———

John Lennon
Singer - Song Writer

A parting thought

A parting thought

I hope you have found this book to be a useful guide towards taking your leap or making changes in your life.

I wanted to leave you with a sentiment from Eckhart Tolle. Because whilst I am (of course) a huge advocate of helping people to achieve the things they want to achieve in life, I also think there is a balance to be struck between appreciating the here and now, whilst also designing your ideal future life. Eckhart Tolle describes this beautifully.

We plan these big things, and then pay little attention to the intervening periods whilst we wait for the big things to happen. Holiday. Promotion. Perfect partner. Business launched. Book written.
(I'd include 'leap taken' in that list).

The irony is, most of your life IS the intervening periods**. And yet we spend these periods waiting for the big thing that is in the future to happen, and we miss the now.**

Give attention to what you are doing now, so that what you are doing now, is not just a means to an end Give attention to what you are doing now, so that what you are doing now, is not just a means to an end.

Give attention to what you are doing now, so that what you are doing now, is not just a means to an end.

Eckhart Tolle
Author & Spiritual Teacher

So for me, the key here is not to try with grim determination to achieve your leap, but to enjoy the process of getting to the leap, as much as the end result of the leap itself. Enjoy getting to know yourself again! Enjoy every step. Because every step is a step closer than you were, to **being more you and finding that career you'll love!**

A sneaky extra bit

WHAT IS COACHING?

Coaching is a series of exploratory conversations that can help you to make changes in your life. Coaching also involves you completing activities between conversations to try out experiments in how you behave, make observations and carry out research. All of which can then be discussed in the next coaching conversation. The tools in this book are the ones I give my clients to complete between coaching sessions.

The conversations you have with a coach are like no other conversations you will have with anyone else!

No matter how great your friends, family, partner or work colleagues are, there's always some sort of dynamic going on in those relationships that prevents a truthful and truly transformational conversation to occur. Whereas with a coach, it's much easier to tell them what you can't tell anyone else.

FIVE REASONS WHY COACHING CAN HELP YOU

1. The purpose of a coach: My purpose as a coach is to totally understand you, so that I can help you. Therefore, I will be focused on what you think and feel, and what is important to you. In my attempt to understand you (by asking questions to explore what you say and do), you will begin to understand yourself better. As you explain to me the thoughts and concepts in your head (that sit slightly below your conscious awareness until asked to express them), you'll start to get clarity or be able to challenge your thinking.

2. The way a coach listens: In no other conversation in your life will you be listened to the way a coach will listen to you. Most people only half listen, often with judgement and the intent to respond and give a solution. Whereas a coach listens with curiosity and the intent to fully understand you.

3. A coach believes the answers lie within you: I see my job as helping you to clarify what you want, as well as helping to remove the barriers that have been getting in your way. A coach won't tell you what to do, they will help build your skills in self-awareness, self-management and self-belief to figure things out and take action yourself.

A coach listens by:	Believing that:
Giving unconditional positive regard	You're pretty cool just for being you
Being non-judgementally curious	Life is complex
Giving space for you to speak	You have the answers
Playing back what you've said	It's important you feel understood

4. You can tell a coach stuff you can't tell anyone else: This is because the dynamics are different in a coaching relationship. It's often hard to tell the truth to others about how you feel. But being able to talk about what's really going on in a non-judgmental and safe way with a coach, is so important when trying to make changes. Sometimes simply saying something out loud to someone you trust and not being judged for it, can help you move past the impact it is having on you.

5. Accountability maintains focus: Regular meetings with a coach can help you remain focused on the changes you want to make for yourself. It's so easy to get distracted by all the things you have to do in your day to day life, and then take your eye off the important changes you want to make. Therefore, knowing you have a coaching session coming up can help keep you on track.

HOW TO CONTACT ME

I offer one to one and group coaching programmes for people stuck at a career crossroads, and I also offer coaching to other executive coaches.

So if you would like to find out more about me and my coaching programmes, or if you have any questions about what you have read in this book, or if you would like to find out how you can complete a Strengthscope questionnaire, then please feel free to contact me or connect with me:

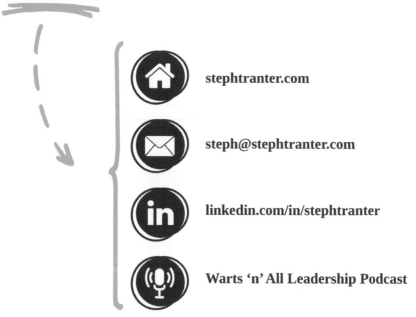

stephtranter.com

steph@stephtranter.com

linkedin.com/in/stephtranter

Warts 'n' All Leadership Podcast

Further reading & resources

THE ELEMENT - Sir Ken Robinson
If you only read one book in this list, then make it this one. It will revolutionise how you see yourself and your uniqueness.

THE HAPPINESS ADVANTAGE - Shawn Achor
This book is full of robust research that provides the credibility behind positive psychology and how it can help you reach your potential.

YOUR BRAIN AT WORK - David Rock
This book focuses on understanding how you can more productively harness the different systems in the brain to enable you to be more effective at work and in life.

WISE MIND LIVING - Dr Erin Olivio
This book can help you to understand more about the emotion families, and offers practical ways for you to manage them.

MINDSET - Dr Carol Dweck
This book goes through the research carried out by Dr Carol Dweck, and the insights she obtained about holding a Growth Mindset.

BIG MAGIC - Elizabeth Gilbert
This book is all about tapping into your creativity, but I also believe it contains some great insights into how to be more you.

TED TALKS:
Do schools kill creativity? - **Sir Ken Robinson**
The power of believing that you can improve - **Dr Carol Dweck**
The happy secret to better work - **Shawn Achor**

Courage doesn't always roar. Sometimes courage is the quiet voice **at the end of the day, saying, I will** try again **tomorrow.**

———

Mary Anne Radmacher
Writer & Artist

Acknowledgements

Acknowledgements

Thank you to my sister Alison Lincoln who gave me my very first self-help coaching book, called 'Weekend Life Coach' by Lynda Field. This book set me on the course that led me to the place I am now in. Without that gift I don't think I would be where I am today, doing what I love and working in a way that works for me.

Thank you to my Mum Pat Tranter, and my Dad Peter Tranter for their continued interest and support in my work.

Thank you to Dr Paul Brewerton and James Brook for the belief they both had in me when I first started my business, as well as of course giving me my first ever bits of freelance consultancy work at Strengthscope. Thank you also to David Lincoln and the rest of the team at Strengthscope who continue to inspire and support me with their fabulous strengths-based tools.

Thank you to so many friends and colleagues who have supported me along the way. Your words, warmth, wisdom and unwavering belief in me has kept me grounded, inspired, resilient, and most of all, true to myself, especially at times when I have lost my way. So a heartfelt thank you to: Emma Smith, Caroline Roodhouse, Debbie Jenssen, Penny Wallace, Sam Oliver, Claire Ingle, Alison Warner, Hector Riva-Palacio, Sarah Makinde, Ray Charlton, Alan Oram (and everyone at Alive with Ideas), Dan Benham, Zara Bates, Sarah Ellis, Lisa Wainwright MBE, Gary Lomas, Sarah Sangster, Paul Matthews, Amanda Bennett, Lorna Mitchel, Rachel Parsonage, Sarah Hemus, Alex Green, Brad Soloman, Nina Baum, Emma Ware, Mike Byford, and Jonny Jacobs.

A special thank you to the following wonderful humans for proofreading and reviewing my book - Alison Lincoln, Peter Tranter, Pat Tranter, Emma Smith, Dr Paul Brewerton, Caroline Roodhouse, Debbie Jenssen, Helen Deverell, Andy Rivers, Jayne Kavanagh, Paul Hillan, Gavin Oates, Brad Soloman, Rachel Parsonage, Sue Anstiss MBE, Carly and Daniel Avener, Amanda Bennett, Mark Thomas, Lorna Mitchel, Karena Thomas, Annamarie Phelps CBE OLY, Mark Boyle and Jane Storm.

Thank you to Alan Oram, Director and Founder of Alive with Ideas, and lifelong friend, for his creative genius and dedication to creating a front cover that makes me beam every time I look at it. Thank you also to the team at Alive with Ideas who helped create and refine the design of this book.

A very special thank you to Valentina Zagaglia of Alive with Ideas for pulling everything together and making the whole design of the book something very beautiful and special.

Finally, a very important thank you to Colin Russell, who in 2010 said to me three simple words - 'You should coach!'. This changed forever my belief in what I was capable of doing and being. Thank you!

Printed in Great Britain
by Amazon

25210380R00087